# THE STEAMING SIXTIES

## Stirring episodes from the last decade of Steam on BR

## 12. Central Wales

## Text and photographs by Terence Dorrity


ISBN-978-1-906919-83-2
First published in 2015 by Irwell Press Ltd., 59A, High Street, Clophill, Bedfordshire, MK45 4BE
Printed by Akcent Media, UK

For the purposes of this book 'Central Wales' has been used loosely to cover the British Railways lines in the counties (as they then were) of Merionethshire, Montgomeryshire and Cardiganshire. These lines were part of the Western Region until the introduction of the winter timetable in September 1963 when, with the exception of the route from Aberystwyth to the south, they were transferred to the London Midland Region. They were predominantly formerly Cambrian Railways lines and this explains why, although just over the border into England, we start at Oswestry in Shropshire because this was where the headquarters and works of the Cambrian Railways were situated, and so much of the work of the locomotives allocated there was in Wales. The Cambrian was absorbed into the Great Western Railway at the grouping in 1923. Before that the GWR had already operated lines linked with the Cambrian; at Aberystwyth towards the south to Carmarthen, from Dolgelly to Ruabon and beyond, and at Oswestry. The old county town of Cardigan is right at the south of the county and it was the terminus of a branch from Whitland. One narrow gauge line that had belonged to the Cambrian, the Vale of Rheidol, was operated by British Railways at the time I took these photographs. Another ex-Cambrian narrow gauge concern was the Welshpool and Llanfair, also still in reality a British Railways line since, from late 1962 until it was purchased in 1974, it was leased by the preservation society that now runs it. Three other lines, the Talyllyn, Ffestiniog and Snowdon Mountain railways, are also represented in this book because, although private or preserved, they figured in the BR passenger timetables of the time. Not far away were the narrow gauge slate quarry railways, many locomotives of which are now fortunately preserved, and the main ex-LNWR North Wales main line to Holyhead; but that is another story.

The photographs are shown in more or less geographical sequence starting at Oswestry, going along the Cambrian main line to Machynlleth and Dovey Junction before branching first south to Aberystwyth and down to Cardigan and then north along the coast from Dovey Junction, with the Ruabon and Dolgelly line joining at Morfa Mawddach. Finally there is a visit to the three neighbouring non-BR narrow gauge passenger lines.

The engine shed codes in the area were changed in 1963 when the London Midland Region took control and, where mentioned in this book, are the ones that applied on the date the photograph was taken. Fortunately, I kept detailed notes at the time I took the photographs but I found the following useful for additional information:

The relevant British Railways Western Region and London Midland Region timetables.

BR steam locomotive index: www.brdatabase.info

Rail UK: www.railuk.info

Six Bells Junction: The Railtour Files: www.sixbellsjunction.co.uk

The websites of the preserved lines mentioned.

**Terence Dorrity 2015**

7822 FOXCOTE MANOR at Aberystwyth shed on Saturday 13 July 1963.

Ex GWR C. B. Collett-designed 7812 ERLESTOKE MANOR pulls out of Oswestry station on the 11:25 Saturdays-excepted all stations Oswestry to Whitchurch service on Tuesday 4 August 1964. It is interesting to note the complex layout and multiple platforms of this once-important station which lost its through passenger services to Welshpool and beyond on 18 January 1965. A shuttle service to the main line at Gobowen continued until 7 November 1966 when the station was closed. Cambrian Heritage Railways are working towards restoring the line from Oswestry to Gobowen and for some distance along the line south towards Pant.

Another Manor, 7807 COMPTON MANOR, approaches Oswestry on a goods train coming from the Gobowen direction at midday on Tuesday 4 August 1964. The picture was taken from Whittington Road. The mound of Oswestry Iron Age fort, now managed by English Heritage, can be seen in the background. This locomotive was built at Swindon in 1938 and it was withdrawn for scrapping three months after this photograph was taken, in November 1964.

Hawksworth-designed light pannier tank 1668 shunting at Oswestry on Tuesday 4 August 1964. Although a GWR design, all seventy of the class were built at Swindon Works by British Railways after nationalisation. 1668 entered service in 1955 and was withdrawn, from Oswestry shed, just ten years later, in 1965.

Three years earlier, on Thursday 17 August 1961, another 16XX pannier tank, 1628 (built at Swindon Works in 1950) stood at Oswestry shed (89D) in front of Collett-designed 57XX pannier tank 3600, built in 1938. 1628 was withdrawn, after sixteen years service, in September 1966 and 3600 in December 1963. Both were scrapped. Alongside is Ivatt Class 2 mogul 46527 which, like 1628, was also built after nationalisation by BR at Swindon, in 1953. It was withdrawn in October 1965.

On the same day, Thursday 17 August 1961, 7801 ANTHONY MANOR was also on Oswestry, its home depot. It was built at Swindon Works in 1938 and withdrawn in July 1965 and scrapped. This light class of 4-6-0 locomotives was particularly suitable for hauling trains on the former Cambrian Railways main lines.

14XX 0-4-2T 1440 was on Oswestry shed too on Thursday 17 August 1961. Looking well groomed it was still sporting the early British Railways 'Lion on a cycle' emblem which was the style used from 1948 until 1956 when it was replaced by a lion holding a wheel. 1440 was built at Swindon Works in March 1935 as Great Western 4840. It was withdrawn from service at the end of 1963 and scrapped.

Ivatt 2-6-0 46515 on Oswestry shed, by then re-coded 6E, on Tuesday 4 August 1964. It had been built at Swindon in 1953 and was eventually withdrawn from Wigan Springs Branch (10A) in May 1967 and scrapped. Oswestry shed was closed to steam on 18 January 1965.

Withdrawn 'Dukedog' 4-4-0 9017 inside Oswestry Works on Thursday 17 August 1961. This class used parts of earlier 'Duke' and 'Bulldog' classes, hence the strange nickname. 9017 entered service as 3217 in 1938. It had been allocated the name EARL OF BERKELEY but this was never carried as the 'Earl' names were transferred to more prestigious Castle class 4-6-0s. It was withdrawn in October 1960 but fortunately was bought for preservation and can now be seen at the Bluebell Railway, Sussex. This was the Cambrian Railways works; it closed in November 1966 but protected by grade two listed status it is still standing. Among other uses it serves as a health centre.

Ivatt 2-6-0 46512 at Llanymynech station, right on the border between England and Wales, on Tuesday 4 August 1964. A pause in the working of this goods train has afforded a chance for the Fireman to bring some coal forward. The loco was allocated to Oswestry shed (re-coded to 6E in 1963). Built at Swindon in 1952 and withdrawn in December 1966, it was later bought from Woodham Bros Barry scrapyard and is now preserved on the Strathspey Railway where it has been given the name E.V. COOPER, ENGINEER.

Another Ivatt 2-6-0, 46516, arrives at Carreghofa Halt, Llanymynech, on a local passenger train on the Llanymynech to Llanfyllin branch on Tuesday 4 August 1964. It was the 12:55 (Saturdays excepted) from Llanymynech which was due to arrive at Llanfyllin at 13:20. This short (8½ mile) branch was opened in 1863, primarily to convey limestone from the quarries. It was closed in January 1965.

46516 has now just left Carreghofa Halt with the local. The picture was taken from the Ellesmere Canal and B4398 road bridge. 46516 had entered service early in 1953 and was withdrawn in May 1967 and scrapped. It was allocated to Oswestry shed (6E). The canal was the Llanymynech branch of the Ellesmere Canal but it has now been categorised as part of the Montgomery Canal.

Welshpool and Llanfair Railway 2ft 6in gauge 0-6-0T No.1 THE EARL, built by Beyer Peacock Ltd of Gorton (Manchester) in 1902 with the works number 3496, at Castle Caereinion on Saturday 9 June 1962. It was renumbered 822 by the Great Western. The W&L was still a British Railways line, though it had closed to traffic in November 1956 and its two locomotives stored at Oswestry Works. 822 was officially withdrawn by BR in August 1961 but in fact it had been returned to the line during the previous month. The Welshpool and Llanfair Light Railway Preservation Company leased the line from British Railways from late 1962 until it was purchased outright in 1974. By the time this photograph was taken the locomotive had regained its original number.

The other Welshpool and Llanfair Beyer Peacock 0-6-0T of 1902, No.2 COUNTESS, in action on 4 August 1964. The preserved line had begun operation from Llanfair Caereinion on 6 April 1963. COUNTESS is at Sylfaen, where trains had just started to run to on the recently opened extension. Before that trains had terminated at Castle Caereinion, the station before. COUNTESS had the works number 3497 and had been renumbered 823 by the Great Western Railway. Both locos can still be seen working on the line.

7812 ERLESTOKE MANOR near Buttington Junction, Welshpool, with the 'Cambrian Coast Express', on Friday 2 July 1965. The train had left Aberystwyth at 9:50, joining with the 8:20 Pwllheli section at Dovey Junction, and was due to arrive at London Paddington at 16:00. This locomotive was built at Swindon in 1939 and was withdrawn in 1965 but it is now preserved and based at the Severn Valley Railway.

7824 IFORD MANOR on the 14:45 Aberystwyth to Oswestry (arrive 18:06) running 25 minutes late at Carno on Saturday 15 August 1964. The roughly chalked headcode and the unloved appearance of the locomotive were indicative of the decline in standards that had started. 7824 was built at Swindon in 1950 and withdrawn in November 1964. Carno station was closed to passengers in 1965 but there is a local campaign to reopen it. The station building became part of the Laura Ashley factory from 1967 until that closed in its turn in 1985.

Oswestry's BR Standard class 4 2-6-4T 80132 on the 16:25 Newtown to Machynlleth (arrive 17:20) local passenger train at Carno station, exchanging tokens on Saturday 15 August 1964. Oddly, this train was shown in the London Midland Region summer timetable as Saturdays excepted but apparently it ran anyway, as it was also timetabled to do in the following winter timetable. It should have crossed with the 14:45 Aberystwyth to Oswestry earlier at Caersws but the latter was running late. 80132 entered service in 1956 and was withdrawn in January 1966.

Machynlleth's BR Standard class 4 4-6-0 75004 works hard to surmount Talerddig bank on the Saturday only 7:20 departure from Pwllheli to London Paddington (arrive 15:15) train on Saturday 15 August 1964. Apparently the Talerddig cutting, at over 110 feet, was the deepest in the world through solid rock when completed in 1862.

Standard 2-6-4T 80099 pilots 7810 DRAYCOTT MANOR up Talerddig bank on the 'Cambrian Coast Express' on Saturday 15 August 1964. One section of the train had left Aberystwyth at 9:45 and the other had started at Barmouth (not at Pwllheli as on weekdays) at 9:10. They had combined at Dovey Junction and the train was due to arrive at London Paddington at 16:05. DRAYCOTT MANOR was built in 1938 and was withdrawn in September 1964.

Two BR Standard tanks, Brighton-built class 4 2-6-4T 80099 and Swindon-built class 3 2-6-2T 82034, return down Talerddig bank on Saturday 15 August 1964. 80099 was built in 1955 and withdrawn in May 1965. 82034 was built in the same year but survived more than a year longer as it was withdrawn at the end of 1966. Both were scrapped.

7820 DINMORE MANOR attacking the Talerddig bank without assistance on the 'Cambrian Coast Express' on Monday 28 June 1965 – this was the last year to see Manors in BR service on the line. The train had left Aberystwyth at 9:50 and joined the 8:20 Pwllheli portion at Dovey Junction. It was due to arrive at London Paddington at 16:00.

DINMORE MANOR continues past at Talerddig on Monday 28 June 1965. Withdrawn a few months later, this 1950 built locomotive is now preserved on the Gloucestershire Warwickshire Railway.

7822 FOXCOTE MANOR near Llanbrynmair at the start of the Talerddig climb on the combined summer Saturday only 10:45 departure from Aberystwyth and 10:30 departure from Barmouth to Manchester Piccadilly (arrive 16:12) train on Saturday 15 August 1964. Built at Swindon by British Railways in 1950 and withdrawn from service in November 1965, it is now, appropriately, preserved in Wales, on the Llangollen Railway.

Ex-GWR Churchward mogul 6367 approaches Llanbrynmair station on Saturday 15 August 1964 at the head of the peak summer Saturdays only 11:25 Barmouth to Birmingham Snow Hill (arrive 15:54). A BR Standard 2-6-4T awaits its turn to leave on the 8:15 Manchester Piccadilly to Aberystwyth (arrive 14:15).

6367 leaves Llanbrynmair with the Birmingham train some minutes later on Saturday 15 August 1964. 6367 was built at Swindon in 1925 and withdrawn from service just five months after this photograph was taken, in November 1964. The station was closed in 1965.

BR Standard class 4 4-6-0 75002 and 7821 DITCHEAT MANOR approach Llanbrynmair from the Machynlleth direction on the about 25 minutes late Saturdays only 10:35 Pwllheli to Birmingham Snow Hill (arrive 17:23) combined with the 12:48 Aberystwyth to Whitchurch (arrive 16:40) through coaches on Saturday 15 August 1964. At this time both locomotives were allocated to Machynlleth shed (6F). 1951 Swindon-built locomotive 75002 remained in service until August 1967.

7812 ERLESTOKE MANOR near Commins Coch on the 16:09 Pwllheli and 18:05 Aberystwyth to Shrewsbury (arrive 20:57) train on Tuesday 29 June 1965. The two portions had combined at Dovey Junction.

Someone has had a go at cleaning the more easily accessible areas of 80105 so it was looking reasonably presentable despite its missing smokebox number plate on Machynlleth shed (6F) on the following day, Tuesday 29 June 1965. 80105 fared better than 80048; in 1975, it was bought from Woodham's Barry scrapyard by members of the Scottish Railway Preservation Society and restored to working order. It has since worked on a number of preserved lines. Machynlleth shed closed in 1966.

DITCHEAT MANOR was allocated to Machynlleth (89C) at this time. Built by BR in 1950, 7821 was withdrawn in November 1965 but it was saved from the famous Woodham Bros scrap line at Barry in 1980 and it is now preserved.

A little later on Saturday 13 July 1963, DITCHEAT MANOR left Aberystwyth in charge of the 9:45 'Cambrian Coast Express'. The castellated tower on the right was demolished in 1968. This is the site of Plas Crûg, otherwise known as Rheidol Castle. References to what was probably this castle go back to the twelfth century but there was some dispute about the amount of the original fortified building remaining as it had possibly been rebuilt as an eighteenth century folly and much of the site had been incorporated into a farmhouse.

Narrow gauge (1ft 11¾ in) 2-6-2T No.7 OWAIN GLYNDŴR ready for action at the Vale of Rheidol engine shed at Aberystwyth on Tuesday 29 June 1965. No 7, along with no 8 LLYWELYN, was built in 1923 at the Great Western Railway Swindon Works. They replaced two older locomotives on the line which was opened in 1902.

No.9 PRINCE OF WALES was also in steam at the shed on Tuesday 29 June 1965. Later, the VR locomotives were stabled in the main line shed after the end of steam operation there. A new narrow gauge engine shed has now been constructed. No 9 was built at Swindon in 1932 with the number 1213. This was because it was officially a rebuild of a withdrawn V of R locomotive with that number but it was, in reality, practically a totally new one. It was renumbered 9 by BR.

Under the protection of a red flag, OWAIN GLYNDŴR crosses the road out of Aberystwyth station at the start of the 11¾ mile mainly uphill run to Devil's Bridge on Saturday 13 July 1963. At this time the coaching stock was painted in Great Western 'chocolate and cream' livery.

Two years later, on Tuesday 29 June 1965, OWAIN GLYNDŴR was again in charge. Here it is leaving Aberffrwd station on the 10:00 departure from Aberystwyth which was due to arrive at Devil's Bridge at 11:00. This was one of three scheduled stops between the two. There were also four request stops. Aberffrwd water tank can just be seen in the distance. The carriages had by then been repainted green with V R on the sides. Later still, controversially, they and the locomotives carried the corporate BR blue livery.

On Monday 28 June 1965, 75004 has charge of the Pwllheli-bound portion of the 'Cambrian Coast Express'. This train had left London Paddington at 11:10 and had divided into Aberystwyth and Pwllheli sections at Machynlleth. It is now on the scenic single track line running along the wall by the River Dyfi (Dovey) estuary between Dovey Junction and Aberdovey; it was due to arrive at Pwllheli at 18:56.

7802 BRADLEY MANOR heads a goods train towards Machynlleth at the same spot and on the same day. It was built at Swindon Works in 1938 and withdrawn in November 1965. It is now preserved on the Severn Valley Railway.

The alternative route to the coast ran from Ruabon to join the Machynlleth-Pwllheli line at Morfa Mawddach. 7801 ANTHONY MANOR and 2-6-0 7314 double-head a Tallyllyn Railway Preservation Society special at Ruabon on Saturday 29 September 1962. This station, still in use, is on the ex-Great Western line between Wrexham and Shrewsbury and it is sometimes cited as the ideal, if probably impossible to achieve, main line connection with the preserved Llangollen Railway. 7801 and 7314 had taken over the train, which had run from London Paddington behind 6000 KING GEORGE V, for the rest of the journey to Towyn.

The next stop for the Tallyllyn special was Corwen. The Ruabon to Morfa Mawddach line was officially closed to passengers on 18 January 1965 although flooding meant that some sections had closed the previous month. This ex-GWR station, which opened in 1865, is now in private hands but a new one, Corwen East, has been built by the preserved Llangollen Railway as the terminus of its extension to the town.

7801 and 7314 stand next to the signal box at Morfa Mawddach on Saturday 29 September 1962. It had been called Barmouth Junction until 1960. The box was necessary because this was the junction between the line from Machynlleth to Pwllheli and the line from Ruabon and Dolgelly (Dolgellau). The two locomotives had hauled the Tallyllyn special from Ruabon but could not run directly to its destination, Towyn, because the curve in that direction had been closed many years before. The return to London via Welshpool took place overnight and was scheduled to depart from Towyn at 23.30. I had the good fortune to be on this train from and to Birmingham Snow Hill. It was a long day!

7827 LYDHAM MANOR and 'small prairie' 4555 were on a Tallyllyn Railway Special at Towyn on Saturday 26 September 1964. They had hauled the train from Ruabon via Dolgelly and Morfa Mawddach just a few months before the closure of that line. Earlier in the day the train had run from London Paddington to Wolverhampton behind 7029 CLUN CASTLE and from Wolverhampton to Ruabon behind 1011 COUNTY OF CHESTER.

LYDHAM MANOR and 4555 on the Tallyllyn Railway Special at Towyn on Saturday 26 September 1964. Both LYDHAM MANOR and 4555 have been preserved. In fact, Churchward designed 4555 had already been bought for preservation directly from BR at the end of 1963, which explains its GW livery. I was also on this special: another long, but very enjoyable and memorable, day!

2251 class 0-6-0 2286 heads a goods train working wrong line in the Machynlleth direction at Towyn on Saturday 9 June 1962. Built at Swindon in 1936 and withdrawn in September 1964, at the time it was allocated to Machynlleth shed (89C).

Machynlleth's 2-6-2T 82034 and its coaches were reflecting the evening light at Towyn at 18:25 on Saturday 26 September 1964. The train was the 16:05 from Pwllheli to Dovey Junction, where it would join the 18:00 Aberystwyth departure with sections to Shrewsbury and London Paddington. 82034 entered service early in 1955 and was withdrawn in December 1966.

Talyllyn Railway No.2 DOLGOCH waits to depart from Towyn Wharf station on the 13:10 'Centenarian' to Abergynolwyn on Monday 28 June 1965. This train was named to commemorate the centenary of the line that year. DOLGOCH was one of the original locomotives constructed for the 2ft 3in gauge line by Fletcher, Jennings & Co of Whitehaven. An 0-4-0 well tank, it was built in 1866 with the works number 63 and is still in service. The carriage behind is No.17, built by the Metropolitan Carriage and Wagon company in 1898 for the Corris Railway as their coach No.8. It then became GWR No.4992 before being withdrawn and bought in 1930 for use as a private summer house. It was eventually saved for restoration by the Talyllyn Railway in 1958.

Talyllyn Railway No.4 EDWARD THOMAS deserves a special place here because it was originally built for the Corris Railway which became part of the Great Western in 1930 and then, briefly before closure, part of the nationalised British Railways in 1948. It retained the number 4 throughout. Seen hear near Brynglas on Monday 28 June 1965, this 0-4-2 'Tattoo' class saddle tank was built in 1921 by Kerr, Stuart & Co Ltd with the works number 4047. It was purchased by the Talyllyn in 1951 and was named EDWARD THOMAS after the former long-serving manager of the railway. Its Giesl ejector, fitted instead of a conventional chimney and carried for about ten years, can be seen in this photograph.

The then-centenarian Ffestiniog Railway PRINCE, an 0-4-0ST built by George England in 1863, starts its run across the Cob by Boston Lodge works on Saturday 13 July 1963. At this time the line only ran from Tan-y-Bwlch to Portmadoc (Porthmadog). It would be another nineteen years before the diversion around the Tanygrisiau reservoir and the gradual opening of sections of the line to Dduallt and beyond would allow running all the way to Blaenau Ffestiniog in 1982.

Ffestiniog Railway No.10 MERDDIN EMRYS, an 0-4-4-0 double Fairlie articulated locomotive built by the railway at their Boston Lodge works in 1879, pulls into Minffordd station on Thursday 1 July 1965.

Ffestiniog 2-4-0ST LINDA, built by the Hunslet Engine Co in 1893 at Portmadoc on Sunday 10 April 1966. It was originally an 0-4-0 saddle tank working at Penrhyn slate quarries on the Port Penrhyn 'main line' and was one of two bought by the Ffestiniog Railway in 1962. LINDA was converted to its present form with a tender from WELSH PONY. It was named after Linda Blanche Douglas-Pennant, daughter of the 3rd Baron Penrhyn.

Snowdon Mountain Railway No.3 WYDDFA and No.7 AYLWIN at Llanberis shed on Wednesday 30 June 1965. No.3, built in 1895, is one of the original 0-4-2 tank locomotives. WYDDFA is the Welsh name for Snowdon. No.7 is part of the second, superheated, batch of 0-4-2Ts, built in 1923. In 1978 it was renamed RALPH SADLER, after the railway's consulting engineer. It is now known simply as 'Ralph'. Both locomotives were built by the Swiss Locomotive and Machine Works of Winterthur for the 2ft 7½ in gauge Abt rack and pinion system line. They have inclined boilers suited to the steep gradients of the line.

No.5 MOEL SIABOD, another earlier type Swiss Locomotive and Machine Works 0-4-2T, on the viaduct near Hebron station on Wednesday 30 June 1965. MOEL SIABOD, named after a nearby peak, was built in 1896.